Seven Favorite Holiday Duets

With

Santa Claus

Parade of the Wooden Soldiers
Toyland
Santa Claus
We Gather Together
I Wonder As I Wander
Chanukah
Jingle Bells

Arranged by
Geoff Haydon and Jim Lyke

Parade of the Wooden Soldiers

Secondo

Music by LEON JESSELL
arr. by Geoff Haydon and Jim Lyke

March tempo ($\quad$ = c. 92)

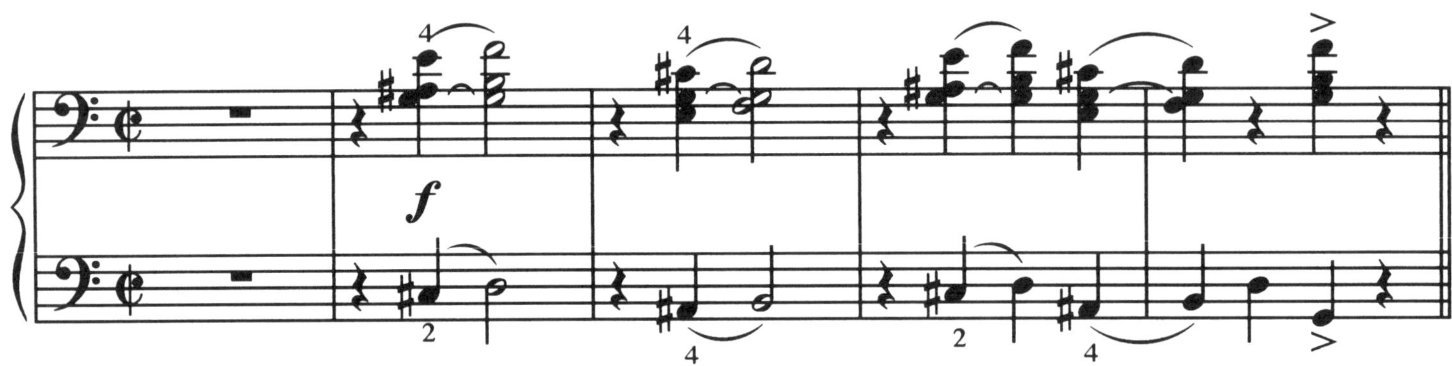

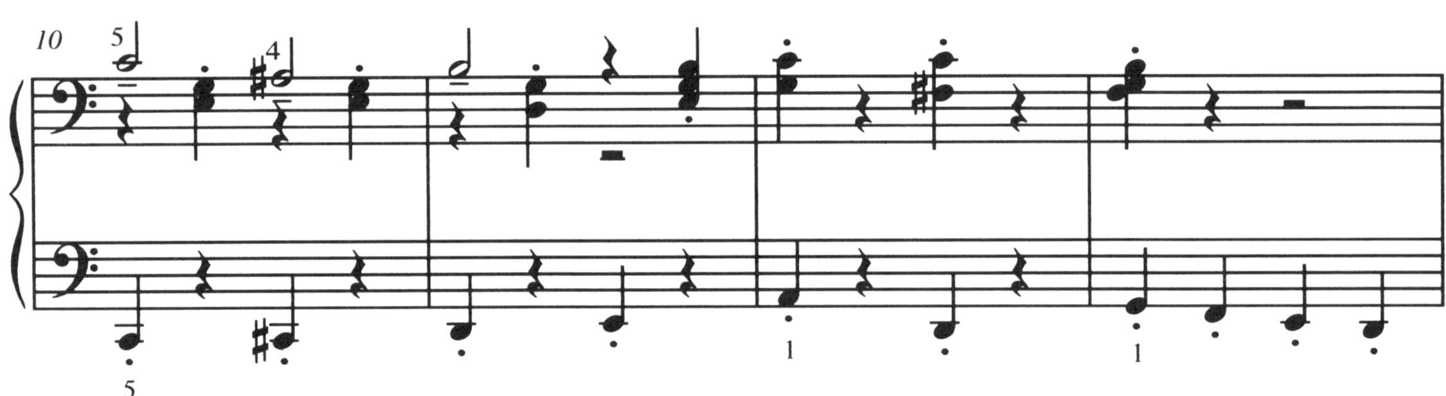

Parade of the Wooden Soldiers

Primo

Music by LEON JESSELL
arr. by Geoff Haydon and Jim Lyke

March tempo (♩ = c. 92)

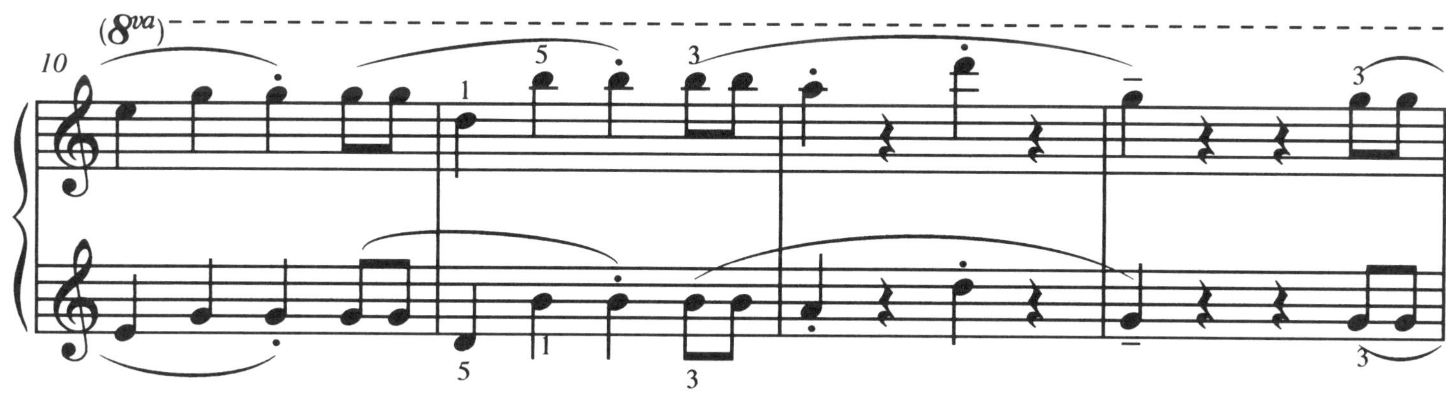

Secondo

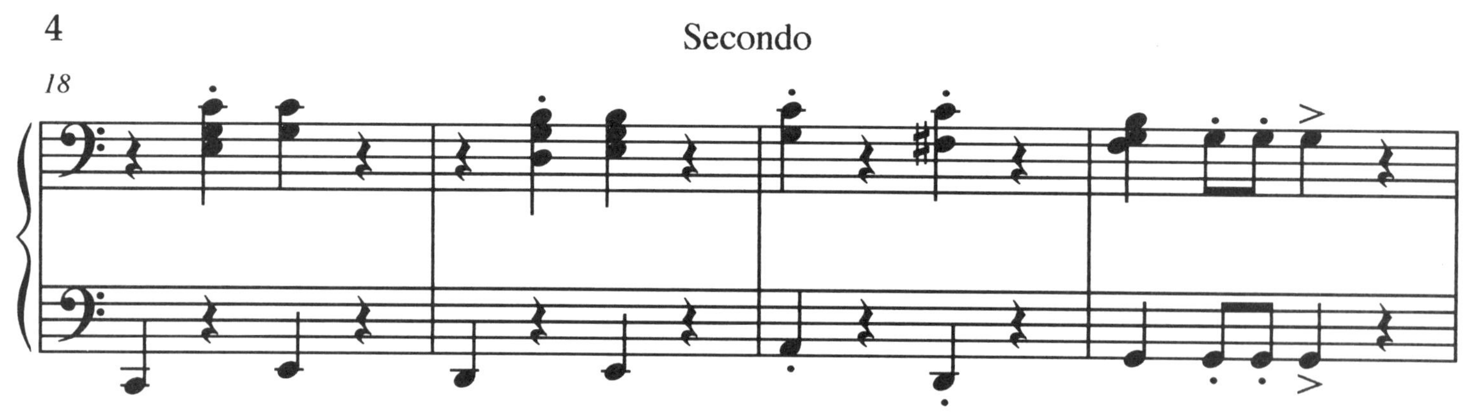

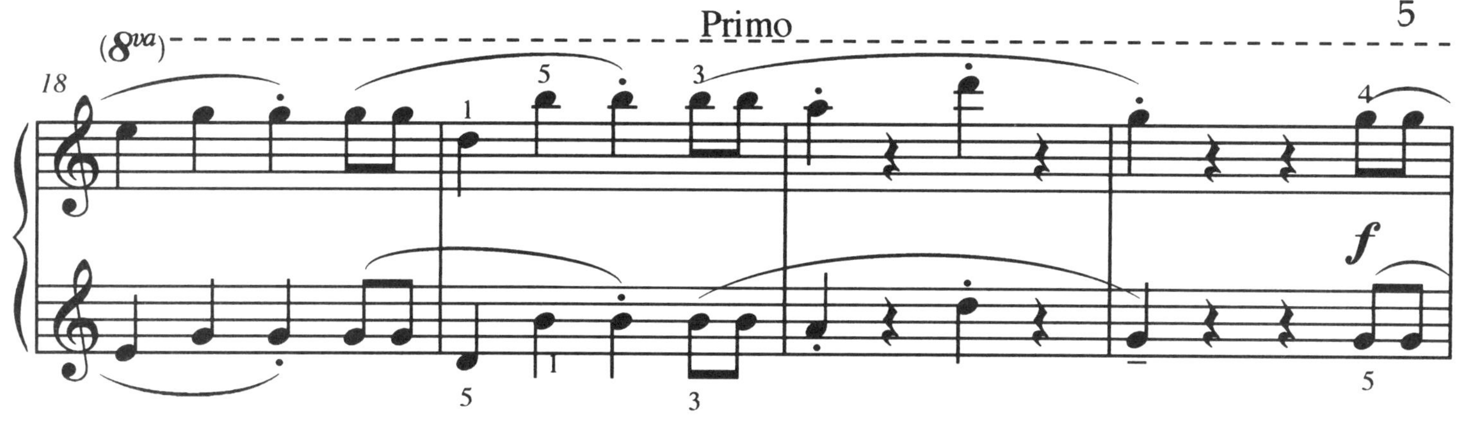

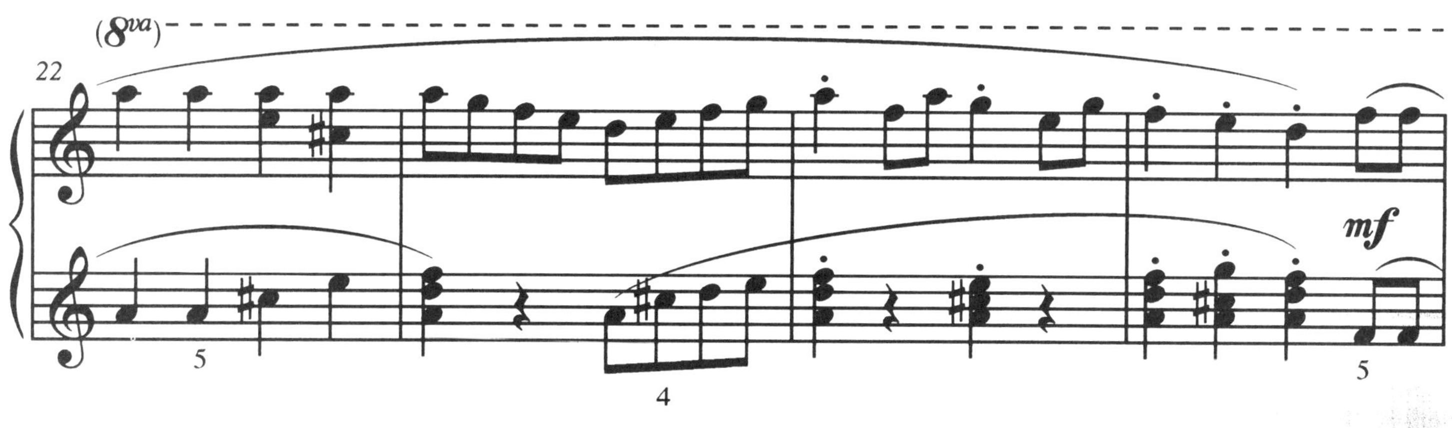

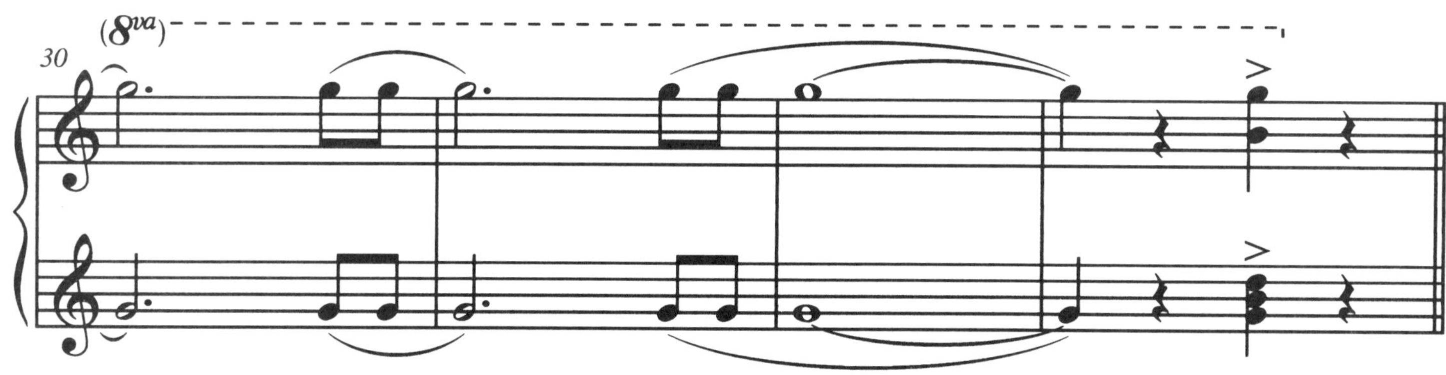

6

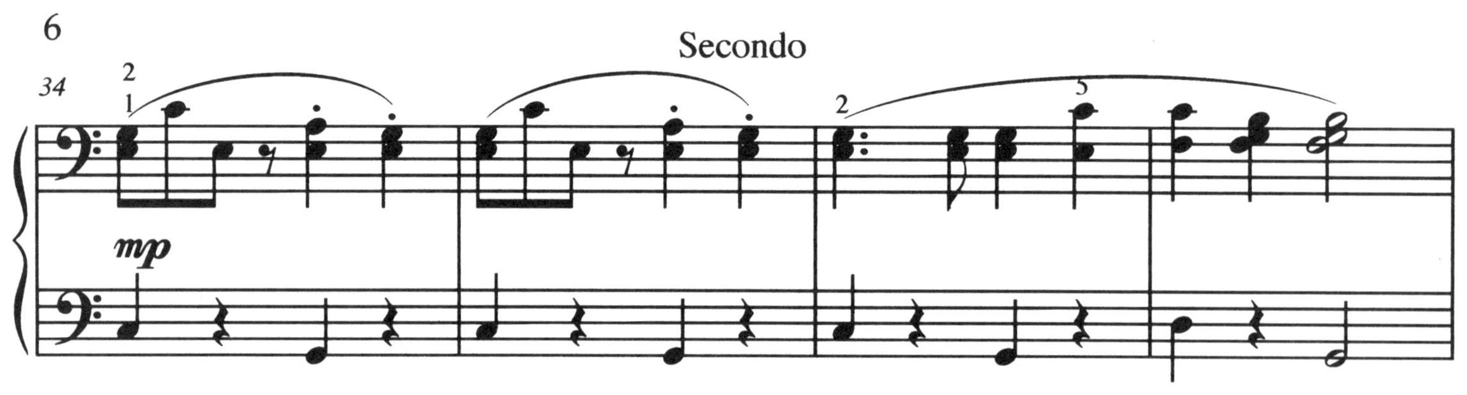

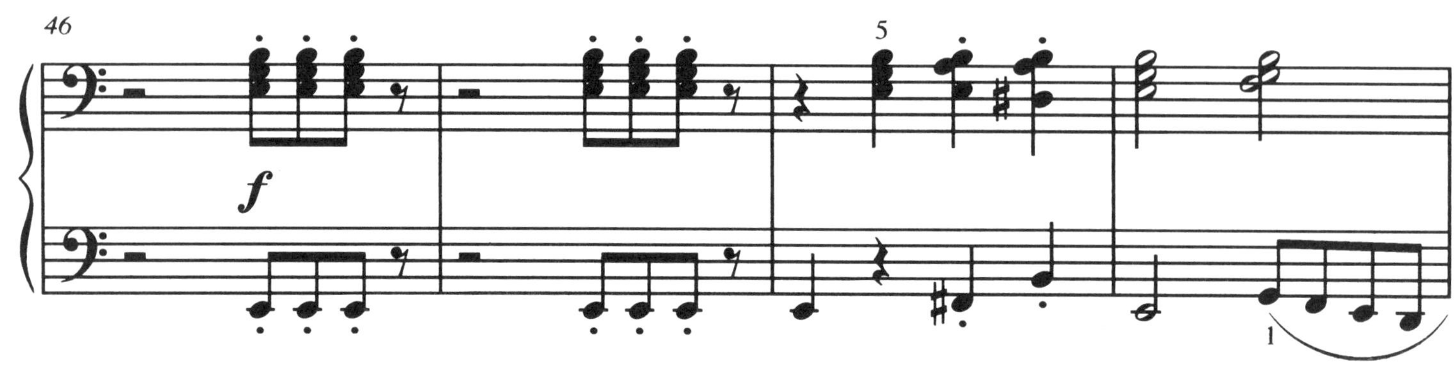

2399

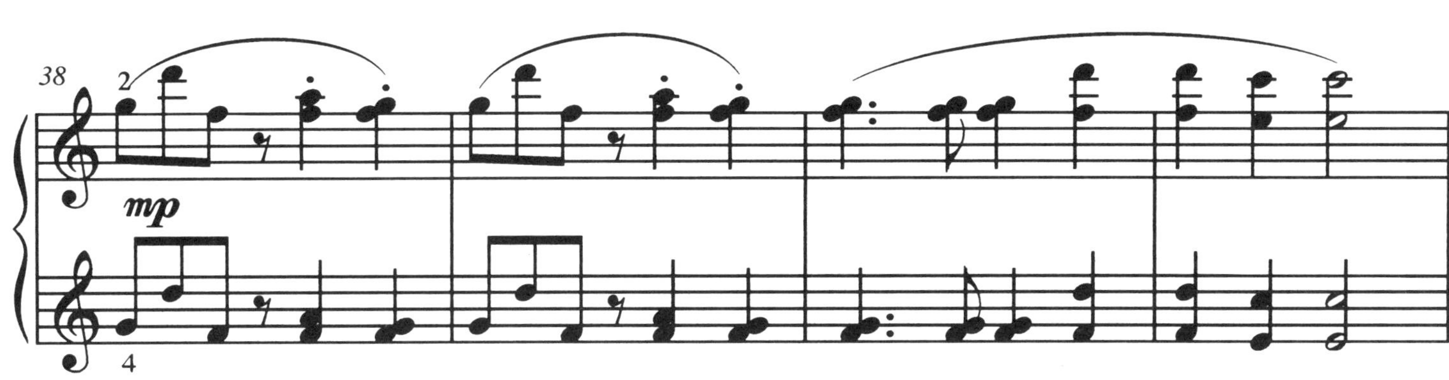

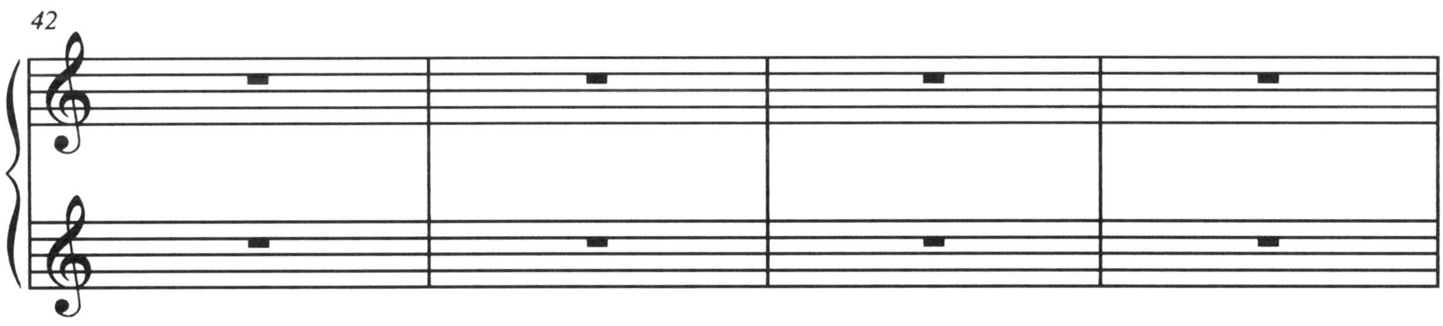

Secondo
50
mf
54
58
62
66
f
ff
2399

2399

Toyland

Secondo

Music by Victor Herbert
arr. by Geoff Haydon and Jim Lyke

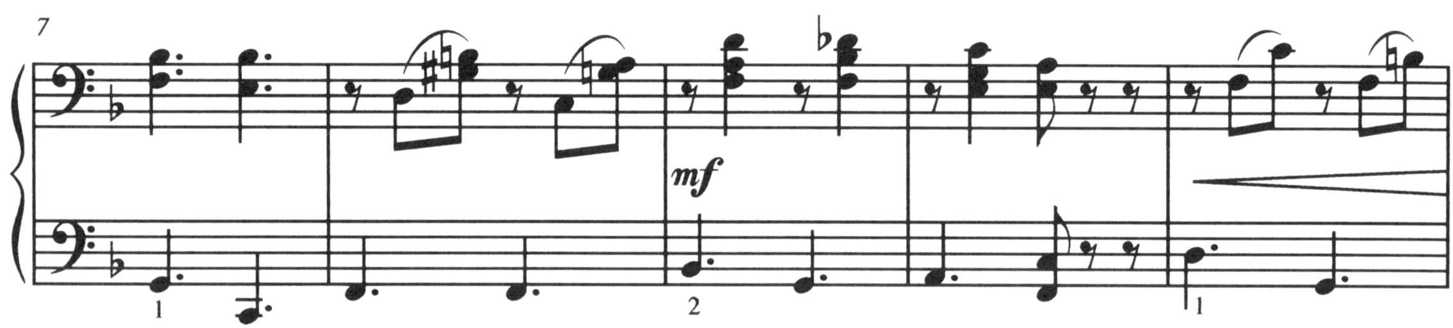

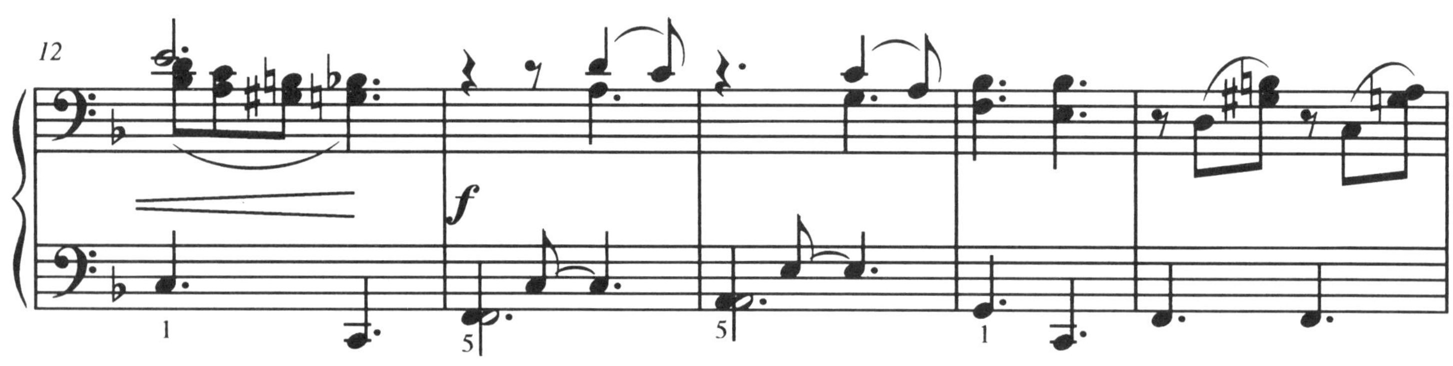

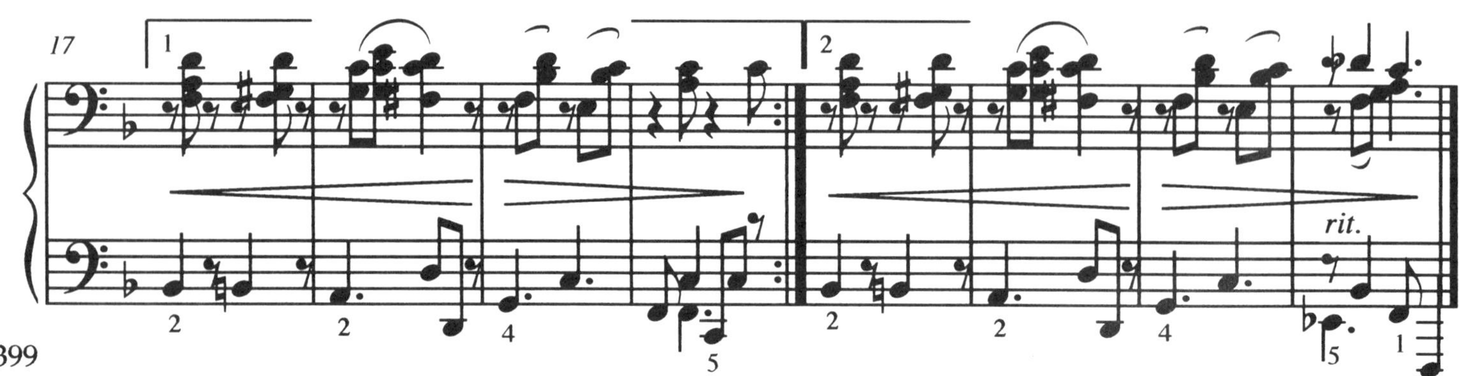

Toyland

Primo

12
CD Tracks
7, 8, 9
28, 29, 30
45

Santa Claus
Secondo

Music by Irving Berlin
arr. by Geoff Haydon and Jim Lyke

Spirited (M.M. ♩ = c. 72)

f

5

mf

9

13

2399

Santa Claus

Primo

Music by Irving Berlin
arr. by Geoff Haydon and Jim Lyke

17
Secondo
4
5
21
5
4
5
4
f
25
1
2
1
29
mf
33
5
3
3
4

Primo
f
mf
2399

Secondo

37
f
41
mp
45
mf
49
f
8va

We Gather Together

Secondo

Anonymous
arr. Geoff Haydon and Jim Lyke

Moderato (♩ = c. 120)

We Gather Together

Primo

Anonymous
arr. Geoff Haydon and Jim Lyke

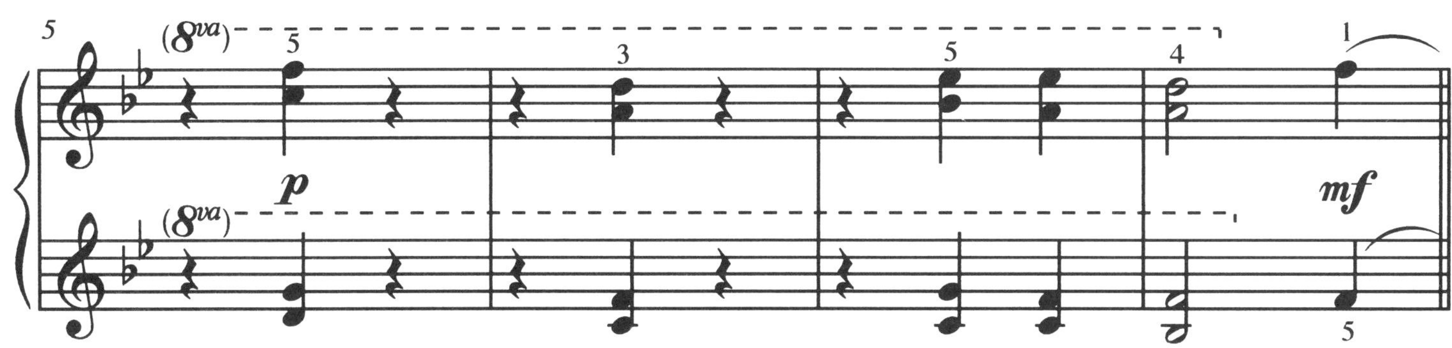

2399

Secondo
f
mf
mp
p
pp
2399

Primo

I Wonder As I Wander

I Wonder As I Wander

Primo

Appalachian Carol
arr. by Geoff Haydon and Jim Lyke

Slowly with expression

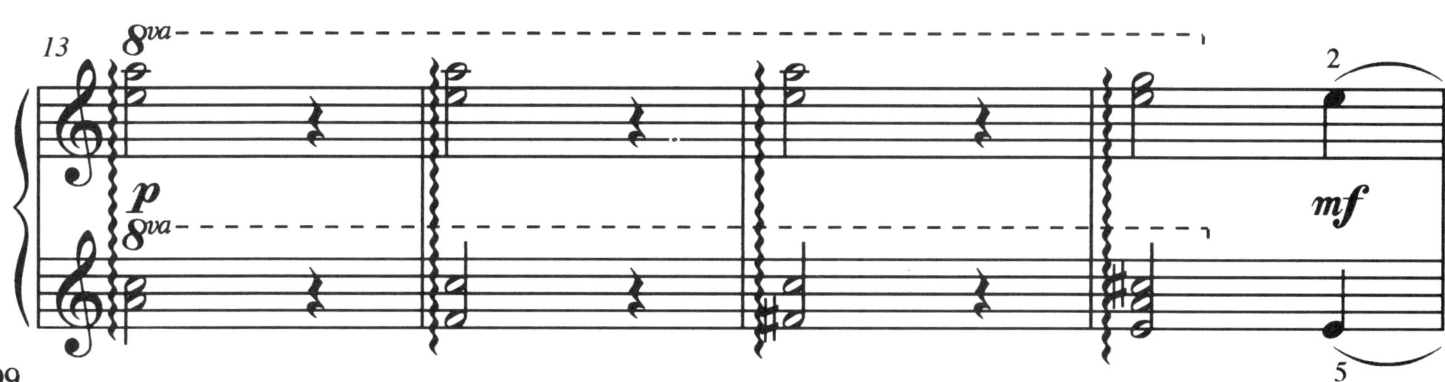

Secondo

Primo

Chanukah

Secondo

Traditional
arr. by Geoff Haydon and Jim Lyke

Chanukah

Primo

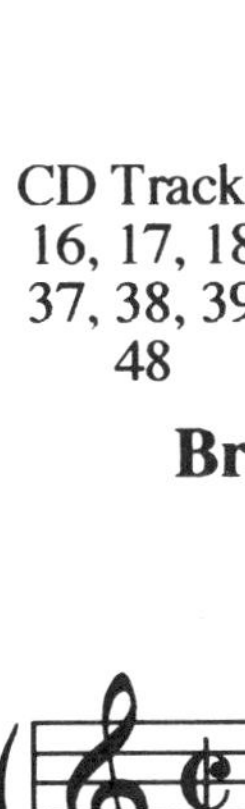

Jingle Bells

Secondo

Music by James Pierpont

arr. by Geoff Haydon and Jim Lyke

Allegro (M.M. ♩ = c. 120)

Jingle Bells
Primo

Music by James Pierpont

arr. by Geoff Haydon and Jim Lyke

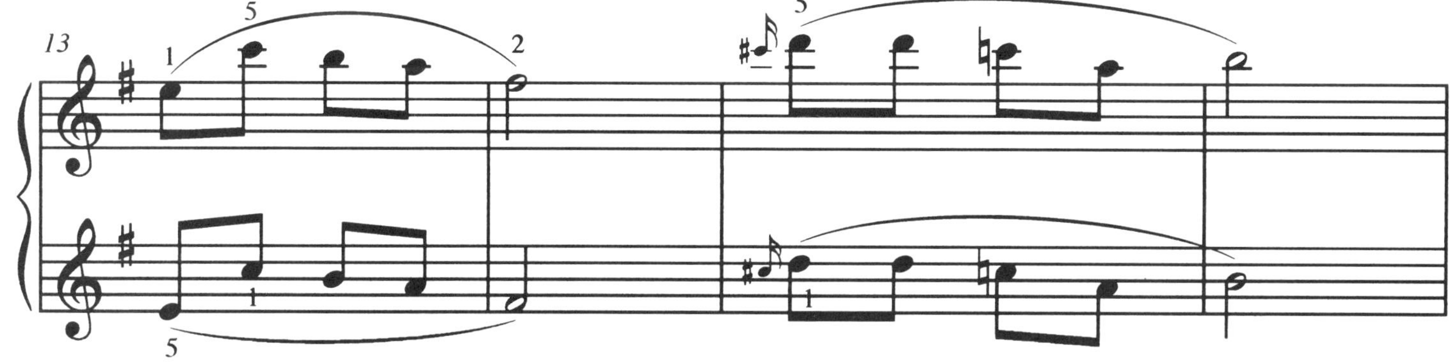

Secondo

Primo

Complete listing in order of the audio tracks on the CD:

Track #

1. Parade of the Wooden Soldiers (Primo + Secondo)
2. Parade of the Wooden Soldiers (Primo)
3. Parade of the Wooden Soldiers (Secondo)
4. Toyland (Primo + Secondo)
5. Toyland (Primo)
6. Toyland (Secondo)
7. Santa Claus (Primo + Secondo)
8. Santa Claus (Primo)
9. Santa Claus (Secondo)
10. We Gather Together (Primo + Secondo)
11. We Gather Together (Primo)
12. We Gather Together (Secondo)
13. I Wonder As I Wander (Primo + Secondo)
14. I Wonder As I Wander (Primo)
15. I Wonder As I Wander (Secondo)
16. Chanukah (Primo + Secondo)
17. Chanukah (Primo)
18. Chanukah (Secondo)
19. Jingle Bells (Primo + Secondo)
20. Jingle Bells (Primo)
21. Jingle Bells (Secondo)
22. Parade of the Wooden Soldiers (Primo, Secondo, + Accomp)
23. Parade of the Wooden Soldiers (Primo + Accomp)
24. Parade of the Wooden Soldiers (Secondo + Accomp)
25. Toyland (Primo, Secondo, + Accomp)
26. Toyland (Primo + Accomp)
27. Toyland (Secondo + Accomp)

Track #

28. Santa Claus (Primo, Secondo, + Accomp)
29. Santa Claus (Primo + Accomp)
30. Santa Claus (Secondo + Accomp)
31. We Gather Together (Primo, Secondo, + Accomp)
32. We Gather Together (Primo + Accomp)
33. We Gather Together (Secondo + Accomp)
34. I Wonder As I Wander (Primo, Secondo, + Accomp)
35. I Wonder As I Wander (Primo + Accomp)
36. I Wonder As I Wander (Secondo +Accomp)
37. Chanukah (Primo, Secondo, + Accomp)
38. Chanukah (Primo + Accomp)
39. Chanukah (Secondo + Accomp)
40. Jingle Bells (Primo, Secondo, + Accomp)
41. Jingle Bells (Primo + Accomp)
42. Jingle Bells (Secondo + Accomp)
43. Parade of the Wooden Soldiers (Accompaniment only)
44. Toyland (Accompaniment only)
45. Santa Claus (Accompaniment only)
46. We Gather Together (Accompaniment only)
47. I Wonder As I Wander (Accompaniment only)
48. Chanukah (Accompaniment only)
49. Jingle Bells (Accompaniment only)